How to Form and Manage Teams Efficiently

How to Form and Manage Teams Efficiently

Table Of Contents

Introduction

Teambuilding and management has become one of the most important elements of success of new businesses. It has become very important to work in unity if any measure of success has to be made.

Here we take a look at how you can ensure that your teams stand the test and achieve the success your company has been hankering for.

Chapter 1:

What Defines a Team?

Summary

What does a team really mean?

What Defines a Team?

Today, 'team' has become a very loosely used word. People are calling any random group of people a team, even in the corporate milieu where it is very important to know what a team is and use it for progress.

A team is not a random group of people. It is a set of people who come together to achieve a particular purpose. A corporate team looks after a particular assignment. A scientific research team tries together to invent or develop something. A sports team tries to win a sports event for their nation or their county or whatever it is that they are representing. Similarly, various teams exist and they can have differing number of members, but these members are all united with a common strand – they are trying to achieve a common goal.

A team is a unique combination of people because, whichever way it is formed, it eventually turns out to be a group of people with _complementary qualities_. This is an essential feature of a team. Thus, in a corporate team, we might have a visualizer, an executor, a thinker, a planner and so on. These people have different merits and that's what keeps them in the team. Their merits are different, but they are aligned in such a way that they complement the merits of other people. This is actually what makes a team a force to reckon with.

We have to realize that we all have our plusses and minuses. None of us are perfect. That is the need to have teams in the first place. When we try to make a team, consciously or unconsciously, we try to unite with people who have talents that we don't have. But our intentions are same. It is just that each one can do a particular job well toward the accomplishment of the goal.

In many cases, teams will need a team leader. The team leader is the cohesive force that keeps the team members together. The job of the team leader is quite essential, in that it is he or she that acts like the glue in keeping the members together. At the same time, the team leader sets and emphasizes upon the goals and ideals for the team.

Chapter 2:

Qualities of Successful Teams

Summary

Let us take a look at the characteristics that every successful team should have.

Qualities of Successful Teams

Here we shall take a look at the main characteristics that a team should possess. If your corporate team does not possess these characteristics, you need to take a closer look at it.

Proper Objectives

The team should have clearly defined objectives. This the purpose with which the team has been set up. Everyone in the team should be aware of these objectives and they must work toward its achievement.

Division of Labor

Though a team is a single mobilized force, every person in the team is a unit contributing in his or her way for the overall functioning of the team. These goals also must be set beforehand, when a member is inducted into the team.

Interaction

Interaction among the team members is important, and this should be healthy interaction. The interaction may be for personal reasons but largely it must be to achieve the purposes that the team as a whole is striving for.

Logical Thinking

There can be no set rules for how a team should think or behave. This depends more on the situation at hand. Due to that, it is imperative that the team members think logically and take rational decisions. The role of the team leader becomes important in this respect.

Acceptance of Majority Decisions

When you put a few people together, it is quite understandable that opinions will differ. Teams cannot sit with these differing opinions though, because decisions need to be taken. A good team will have a sense of adhering to the majority vote.

Compatibility

No team can progress without a feeling of mutual amicability between the members of the team. There must be mutual informality among the members and no disagreements. If there are issues, they must be resolved in a civilized manner.

United Force

A team has to think in unison. This doesn't mean individual members cannot disagree. They sure must, but then they must arrive at common decisions through majority voting methods. But, for all other purposes, there should be a loyal feeling in every member toward the team.

Assessment

It is vital that teams keep evolving. They must meet often just to decide what their achievements have been, what obstacles lay in their path, what shortcomings they have and how to improve upon those. Teams should keep evolving according to changing circumstances.

Chapter 3:

Excite Your Team with Outcomes

Summary

Teams don't sustain themselves for long if they don't see the outcomes. If you are a team leader, you have to keep wowing them with results.

Excite Your Team with Outcomes

No team can persist under a sustained lack of progress. This is true with all kinds of teams, whether it is a corporate team chasing a deadline for an international assignment or it is a major league NBA team. If there are no results, no victories, the team won't stick together. The reason for that is the lack of confidence among the members of the team. Their main intention when they formed the team was to unite with people who had complementary talents to what they have. But when the results don't come, they think that this blend of talents is not working. The team will then dissolve. The members will go apart and either form a new team with new members or completely forget the thing that they were planning to achieve and focus on something else.

Now, if you have a team, you must firmly keep this point in mind. You have to wow your team constantly with results. But what if you don't have results? Here, we don't talk about major victories all the time. No one is so irrational that they expect you to get the President's Medal of Honor for everything that they do as a team. However, you should not ignore the smaller achievements.

Even a single team member doing something that contributes to the team is an achievement. This member has brought the team forward in his or her own way. This is something that can be highlighted. There is no need for open felicitation for everything, but the fact should be brought into the next team meeting. The member in question should be given an acknowledgment of praise. That helps because the member gets motivated. In fact, the entire team gets motivated and they get that important shot in the arm that propels them to keep working.

When the big victories happen, there should be a serious effort in planning a celebration. A celebration isn't a waste of money or time for people in a team – it is a way of acknowledging the fact that the team has worked together in achieving something. It is a collective pat on the back of the team.

Keep wowing your team with results. Big results aren't going to come your way every Sunday, but don't ignore the small things that can help keep the team inspired and motivated.

Chapter 4:

Seek Commitments from Your Team

Summary

Get your teams to make pledges. This helps in keeping the team together and working at achieving common goals.

Seek Commitments from Your Team

An important thing that drives your team is commitment. It is absolutely essential that every person that enters the team makes several commitments, some of which will be obvious and some not so obvious.

The obvious commitments include:-
- → Trying to achieve the common goals that the team is chasing,
- → Participating in the various events that the team pursues, i.e. attending the meetings, workshops, training and orientation sessions, etc.
- → Devoting time for the work of the team, etc.

The non-obvious commitments include:-
- → Getting along with other members of the team,
- → Being loyal to the team,
- → Being innovative and creative in the team efforts so that the team benefits from their thinking,
- → Constantly suggesting improvements and implementing them for the benefit of the team, etc.

When someone is inducted into a team, they have to be told of these commitments and then it becomes highly important for them to stick with them. It becomes essential to make sure that the members keep up with these commitments at all times as well, because if they flounder even temporarily, it could mean a great setback for the team.

So, how do you go about seeking commitments from the team?

(i)   All teams have their own missions, goals and objectives. You must have something of that kind as well, and make sure that you spell out all these objectives to anyone that wishes to get into the team. It could be a good idea to have a sort of swearing-in ceremony when the team is first established and when each new member comes in.

(ii)   At every moment, at least the obvious commitments of the team members should be read again. A member of the team must be made to read these commitments out aloud, and each time it must be a different member.

(iii)   Whenever the opportunity arises, the team leader must make it a point to reinforce the values of the team, even the non-obvious ones.

(iv)   Members shouldn't be encouraged to step out of the line except in extenuating circumstances. One member falling from commitments might mean a big blow to the entire team.

Chapter 5:

Use Teambuilding Activities

Summary

Teambuilding activities help bring the members of the team closer. Without teambuilding efforts, your team might well stay as a staggered bunch of people.

Use Teambuilding Activities

To some level, every team in the world uses teambuilding activities, even if your team contains just two people of which one is you. The natures and scopes of these teambuilding activities might differ, but their intention is the same – to bring the members of the team together. This is the reason teambuilding activities are always participative activities in which every member of the team is expected to come forth and participate. The premise of using these activities is to make people participate and thus find themselves closer to everyone else that are on the team.

When a team is newly set, most teams use an introductory session where everyone introduces themselves and even tell what they can do for the team. This is a definite teambuilding activity. Before the formation of the team, these are just a crowd of people, but after the initial introductions, each one on the team knows what everyone else can do. This is also a point where friendships within the team can be struck. The team members make a mental note of whom to communicate with when they get the next chance.

Further on, you must keep involving other teambuilding activities. If you scan the Internet, you will find tons of teambuilding activities, even games, that can be used to bring team members closer together. These could be organized frequently to set the mood of the team members and to literally 'break the ice'. Know that all team members won't very easily begin communicating with each other. That is the reason you need such icebreakers. They help people in the team to open up to others. When this happens, the communication routes are opened up and it builds the team into a stronger force.

Corporate teams are using such teambuilding activities and even calling professionals to plan such events for their teams. Apart from showing the importance that teams have in the corporate world, this also shows how important teambuilding is. Some corporate organize elaborate events for their teams as well, of which the most popular are paintball competitions which help the team members to really 'open up' to each other.

Chapter 6:

Hiring Professionals to Manage Your Team

Summary

There is professional help available for everything, even for managing teams.

Hiring Professional Help to Manage Your Team

People often ask – is it worth hiring a professional expert to manage teams? For most kinds of teams, the role of a professional is indispensable. For example, a sports coach just cannot be avoided if it is a sports team or a leader just cannot be avoided if it is a corporate team. But we are talking about other kinds of professionals here. Take a look at teambuilding information on the Internet. You will see how people are advertising themselves as 'teambuilding experts' and such other fancy titles.

What do these people purport to do? Teambuilding experts actually help in organizing teambuilding activities within your team which can help the members gel well with each other. They also help in organizing teambuilding icebreaker events which might be helpful in the initial stages of the team's formation to help the members warm up to each other.

However, you will need such kinds of professionals only if you feel that all your efforts to keep your team together have been in vain. And even then, these professionals do not guarantee any success. That may be because they are working with a very serious limitation – they don't know your team as well as you know it. Hence, your efforts at bringing the team closer will probably be more fruitful than the efforts of these experts.

This is what you have to keep in mind if the thought of hiring teambuilding professionals ever crosses your mind. You have to realize that these professionals won't perform supernatural stuff on your team. They will also be working within the same constraints as you are.

The fact is that consistent and proper efforts on your part, as the team leader, can help in keeping your team together in a much better way than anything that a teambuilding professional can do. Just read up on what these experts can do and you will realize that you can do much of the same things, only better.

Chapter 7:

Always Include New People into the Team

Summary

New people bring new energy into the team.

Always Include New People into the Team

Bringing in new people into the team has some great positive benefits that can help the team.

→ It helps the team to stay dynamic. It is great to have new people into a team, even a single new person can mean a healthy bout of energy infused within the team.

→ It is also a good thing for the creativity of the team. New members mean new ideas. It could help the team from stagnating.

→ When new people come into the team, it helps the existing members to get inspired and motivated to do better. There are always mixed sentiments with the inclusion of someone new, ranging from an earnestness to build a new friendship to competition.

However, there are also some pitfalls.

→ The existing members might distrust the new member. This is a natural defensive instinct that we have for something new within our surroundings. Some people might also want to retaliate by fighting back.

→ There might also be a sense of insecurity built within the team. Existing members might think they aren't doing well enough and that's why a new person was brought in.

→ There could be an added pressure on the team to keep up with the ideas and ideologies of the new team members. Since there are bound to be some differences of opinion, the teams might have to change in some way or the other when every new member comes in.

But, let these pitfalls not keep you away from including new members into the team. If you do things right as a team leader, your new member could be nothing other than an asset for the team.

→ Make sure you are clear about why you want this new member in the team. You will mostly owe an explanation to everyone else on the team why you are bringing in new people. If your reasons are correct, people will believe you or else the factor of mistrust will be enormous.

→ Let the new member know each and every existing member of the team properly. Detailed introductions are in order.

→ Spell out the goals and objectives of the team to the new member in front of the existing members so that they feel the new person is going to be just another one among them.

→ Never lay off an existing member and make way for a new member. This causes insecurity among everyone else on the team and performances are affected. If you do have to lay someone off, bring the new member first and let your existing member go after some time.

Chapter 8:

You – The Spinal Cord of Your Team

Summary

Your are the team leader. Your team looks at you with nothing short of reverence. But that will only happen when you are capable in guiding them.

You – The Spinal Cord of Your Team

You are the team leader. You are the one person that has the capacity to keep your team afloat. In fact, a team is only as good as its team leader in most cases. Hence, if you want your team to succeed, you have to take your responsibilities seriously. Here are some of the points that you must inculcate to be a better leader to your team:-

Practice over Precept

This should be your forerunning quality. Team members don't want a preachy leader; they want a leader who can lead them by example. So, don't just talk about doing something, *do it*. Show your team members that things can be done. This is much better than talking them down later on.

Trust

A team leader needs to be trusted. That's vitally important. But how do you gain the trust of others? One way to do that is by remaining truthful to your goals and ideals. If you waver, you are not trusted by your team members. Also, it is important for you to trust your members. Don't go about suspecting everybody. Trust begets trust.

Confidence

Any leader needs to be confident, or at least project himself or herself to be so. If you show even a momentary lack of confidence, you may be belying your team's trust and hope in you.

Inspiring and Motivational

It is also extremely important that you can inspire your team to move toward its goals. This role is all the more crucial when the team is going through a bad patch. It is a good idea to learn how other leaders inspire their teams and emulate some of the good concepts.

Being Receptive

No one likes a leader who is not open to ideas and suggestions. They want to see leaders who can accept new things, even risky ones, or at least to show them a practical side of things. Leaders who are straitjacketed in their methods and those who don't want to evolve don't usually have a long innings.

Chapter 9:

Foster Exchange of Ideas within the Team

Summary

Ideas are the most important resource that a team is built upon.

Foster Exchange of Ideas within the Team

Teams are built on ideas. Though the thing that keeps on driving them is the common goal that they are all chasing, the thing that pushes them till there is the way they can ideate. Actually speaking, ideation is the best thing about being in a team. Teams are made of various people and everyone ideates in their own different way. Since not all of these ideas can be implemented, the route generally adopted by teams is to find the most optimal idea out of all the suggestions that are received. This is what builds an idea that is the most mutually acceptable, and also the most viable.

Building ideas is one of the strengths of being in a team. Individually we might be quite creative, but when we form an idea from the inputs collected from various members in the same team as us, it puts a wholly different spin on things.

That is why, as a team leader, it is one of your utmost priorities to allow as much exchange of ideas in your team as possible. In fact, you must make all effort to foster such exchange of ideas. Several things can happen on account of that:-

→ You get a solution that works for all.

→ You consider the majority opinion, which, in most cases, is also the most optimal solution.

→ You come to know what people in the team are thinking about the situation at hand.

→ You are stimulating the team members to think, and hence they are participating in the efforts of the team.

→ You are encouraging the team members to get closer to each other, which they do when they exchange ideas.

Hence, you must try to make your team ideate as much as possible. Get them together whenever there's a situation that warrants discussion and let them put their heads together. Apart from getting a wonderful solution, you will also get a stronger team.

Chapter 10:

Failures within the Team Doesn't Mean that the Team Has Failed

Summary

Teams don't fail; individuals do.

Failures within the Team Doesn't Mean that the Team Has Failed

It will happen sometime – your team will not be able to meet with the objectives that it has set for itself. It might not be able to meet a deadline or it might not be able to come up with a workable or acceptable solution for a task that was set in front of it. Or, it might be a team that got defeated to some other team. When such things happen, they can put everyone down in the dumps. But one cannot sit brooding over failures, can they?

The first thing that needs to be remembered here is that when a team fails, it is not the failure of each and every person in the team. At least, it is not so in a practical sense. In most cases, a team fails because of a few members in the team. Maybe those members did not put their best foot forward, while the rest of the team members did. Failures of a team are definitely more personal and individualistic than its successes.

So, what can be the solution? The solution is to address the problem and not to blame the team. Blaming the team will also demean the members who really worked hard. Apart from being unfair to them, this will also be detrimental to any future pursuits of the team because these members will harbor a sense of futility in what they do. They will think that even if they give their best shot, someone else is likely to ruin the task once again and they will be taken into the fray too. So, they don't bother giving their best shot at all.

When a team fails, make sure you address the individualistic problem. Your team can still be very good if you find out some solution to this problem. Tackling the problem individualistically reestablishes your trust within the team and you are also able to keep the team working well for future endeavors.

Conclusion

You now have what it takes to make your team put its best foot forward. You can be an efficient team leader and extricate the most optimum output from your team.

Go on, make your team formidable.

All the best to you!!!